Saint Jo____

NE\

AMERICAN
CATECHISM

No. 1

*Prepared in accord with the
"Principal Elements of the Christian Message for Catechesis,"
Chapter V, of the* National Catechetical Directory
approved by the Bishops of the United States.

Primary Grade Edition

Arranged and Explained by
REV. LAWRENCE G. LOVASIK, S.V.D.
Divine Word Missionary

**CATHOLIC BOOK PUBLISHING CO.
NEW YORK**

Dedicated to
SAINT JOSEPH
Patron of the Universal Church

Nihil Obstat: James T. O'Connor, S.T.D.
Censor Librorum

Imprimatur: Joseph T. O'Keefe
Vicar General, Archdiocese of New York

(T-251)

FOREWORD

To the Teacher:

The primary aim of this catechism is to state the official doctrine of the Church, using for the most part the words of the American Bishops in the "National Catechetical Directory" for Catholics of the United States (November 14-17, 1977).

In order to make children familiar with important terminology, and to impress the doctrine of the Church more deeply upon their minds, two methods are used:

(1) *Fill in the blanks*—to choose the correct words found in the answer of the question.

(2) *Can you answer these?*—to ask questions a different way, which will encourage the child to think, using ideas already stated in the official answer. These questions are points for discussion.

Both methods, which can be used for homework, will deepen the knowledge of the child.

The numbers in parentheses refer to the number of the question to enable the child to find the answers with ease.

Stories from the life of Christ, accompanied by pictures, will associate Catholic doctrine with the Word of God.

The material in the Appendices ought to be gradually memorized, since these are fundamental laws and prayers needed in Christian life.

Use visual aids and stories to impress these truths on the minds of your pupils.

Father Lawrence G. Lovasik, S.V.D.

Contents

THE HOLY TRINITY

THE Catholic Church teaches that the mystery we call God, has revealed himself to us as a Trinity of Persons — the Father, the Son, and the Holy Spirit, each equal to each other. There are three Persons in one God.

The mystery of the Trinity is the central doctrine of Catholic faith. Upon it are based all the other teachings of the Church.

Chapter
1 The Holy Trinity

1. What does the history of salvation tell us?

The history of salvation tells us
how God saved us.

2. How do we know about God?

We know about God
because he made himself known to us.

3. How did God make himself known to us?

In the Old Testament of the Bible we read
about God
showing himself to us as the one true God.

4. What is the Bible?

The Bible is the written story of God's
actions in the world.

5. What is the Old Testament?

The Old Testament is that part of the Bible
which was written before the coming of
Christ.

6. What is the New Testament?

The New Testament is that part of the Bible
which tells us about Jesus Christ.
This is called the Gospels.
There are also letters written by the apostles.

7. What did people learn about God in the Old Testament?

In the Old Testament people learned that
  God was real,
that he always did what he promised to do,
and that people could be his friends
if they put their trust in him.

8. How did God make himself known to us in the New Testament?

In the New Testament God made himself
  known to us through his Son, Jesus Christ.

9. What did Jesus teach us about God?

Jesus Christ taught us that in the one God
there are three Persons,
each equal to each other,
Father, Son, and Holy Spirit.

10. What is the mystery of the Trinity?

The mystery of the Trinity
is the one true God in three Persons
— the Father, the Son, and the Holy Spirit.

11. What did Jesus teach us about the Father?

Jesus taught us to love our heavenly Father
because he loves us
and wants to help us in all the needs of our
    body and soul.
He wants to bring us, his children,
to his heavenly home.

12. What did Jesus teach us about himself?

Jesus made himself known to us
as the Son of God
who became man to save us.

13. What did Jesus teach us about the Holy Spirit?

Jesus made known to us
the third Divine Person, the Holy Spirit,
whom the Father and he,
as the Risen Lord, sent to his Church.

14. Why could Jesus teach us about the true God?

Jesus could teach us about the true God because he himself was God.

15. What did Jesus teach his disciples?

Jesus taught his disciples about the true God, and that the Father called them to be his children by giving them his Holy Spirit.

16. How do we become children of God?

We become children of God
through a new life,
the life of our soul,
his own life, which he gives us.

17. How does God give us a share in his own life?

God gives us a share
in his own life
through the gift of
the Holy Spirit.

18. What do we call this life which we receive from God?

We call this life
which we receive from God
sanctifying grace.

19. When do we first receive the life of grace?

We first receive the life of grace
in the sacrament of baptism.

20. How do we honor the Holy Trinity?

We honor the Holy Trinity when we pray to
  God —
the Father, the Son, and the Holy Spirit —
who lives in our soul by grace.

FILL IN THE BLANKS

1. The history of salvation tells us .... (1)

2. We know about God because .... (2)

3. In the .... of the Bible we read about God showing himself to us as .... (3)

4. The Bible is the written story of .... (4)

5. The Old Testament is that part of he Bible which is written before .... (5)

6. The New Testament is that part of the Bible which tells us .... This is called........... There are also letters written by .... (6)

7. In the Old Testament people learned that God was ...., that he always did what .... and that people could be his friends if .... (7)

8. In the New Testament God made himself known to us through .... (8)

9. Jesus taught us that in the one God there are .... Persons, each .... to each other, Fater, ... and .... (9)

10. The mystery of the Trinity is .... (10)

11. Jesus taught us to love our heavenly Father because .... and wants to .... He wants to bring us, his children, to .... (11)

12. Jesus made himself known to us as .... who became .... to ....us. (12)

13. Jesus made known to us the third Divine Persons, the ...., whom the ...., as the Risen Lord, sent to .... (13)

14. Jesus could teach us about the true God because .... (14)

15. Jesus taught his disciples about the ...., and that the Father called them to be .... by giving them .... (15)

16. We become children of God through ...., his own life, the life which he gives us. (16)

17. God gives us a share in .... through the gift of .... (17)

18. We call this life which we receive from God .... (18)

19. We first receive the life of grace in .... (19)

20. We honor the Holy Trinity when ...., the Father, the .... and the ...., who lives in our soul by .... (20)

CAN YOU ANSWER THESE?

1. What is the history of salvation? (1)

2. How do we know that God made himself known to us? (3)

3. What do the Gospels tell us? (6)

4. How did God show his love for people in the Old Testament? (7)

5. What did Jesus teach us about the Blessed Trinity? (9)

6. What did Jesus tell us about his heavenly Father? (11)

7. What did Jesus tell us about the Holy Spirit? (13)

8. What does the new life of grace do for us? (16)

9. What is sanctifying grace? (18)

10. What does the sacrament of baptism give us? (19)

11. Who lives in our soul by grace? (20)

12. What should we do to honor the Blessed Trinity? (20)

THE BAPTISM OF JESUS

JOHN the Baptist came to the desert of Judea and started preaching. "Turn away from your sins," he said, "because the Kingdom of heaven is near! I baptize you with water to show that you have repented, but the one who will come after me will baptize you with the Holy Spirit and fire."

At that time Jesus arrived from Galilee and came to John at the Jordan to be baptized by him. But John tried to make him change his mind. "I ought to be baptized by you," John said, "and yet you have come to me!"

But Jesus answered him, "Let it be so for now. For in this way we shall do all that God requires." So John agreed.

As soon as Jesus was baptized, he came up out of the water. Then heaven was opened to him,

and he saw the Spirit of God coming down like a dove and lighting on him. Then a voice said from heaven, "This is my own dear Son, with whom I am pleased."

The Baptism of Jesus reminds us that there are three persons in one God. Jesus, the Second Person of the Holy Trinity, is baptized. The Spirit of God, who appeared like a dove, is the Third Person, and the Father who spoke about his Son, is the First Person.

It also reminds us that by the Sacrament of Baptism we have become children of God because we were baptized in the name of the Father, and of the Son, and of the Holy Spirit.

Chapter 2   **Worship of God**

21. What must we believe about God?

We must believe that God is all-good, holy, just, and merciful, all-knowing and perfect.

22. How has God shown his love for us?

God has shown his love for us
because he said he would help us;
because he saved us from sin;
because he loves each one of us
and cares for us like a father.

23. When we think of God's love for us, what should we do?

When we think of God's love for us
we should find our joy in him and trust him;
we should honor and worship him.

24. How do we worship God?

We worship God
by offering ourselves to him
through Jesus in the Mass;
by praying to God;
by doing all that he wants us to do;
by using his gifts well to honor him.

25. Why do we worship God especially in Holy Mass?

We worship God especially in Holy Mass
because in Holy Mass Jesus offers himself
    to his Father,
as he did on the cross,
but he does not suffer any more.
He gives God the highest honor and praise.

26. How do we do God's will?

We do God's will by obeying his command-
    ments
and by doing everything we can to please
    him.

27. How do we use God's gifts to honor him?

We use God's gifts to honor him
when we thank him for everything he does
    for us,
and when we pray, work, study, and play
to give him honor.

28. What should we hope for from the goodness of God?

We should hope and pray for
    the help we need
to live a life of love for God
and for our fellow men,
and to be with him in heaven.

29. Why did God put us in this world?

God put us in this world
to know and love him,
to serve him by doing his will,
to get ourselves ready
for the happiness of heaven.

30. How do people show that they do not love God?

People show that they do not love God
when they do not obey him;
when they do not think of him in prayer;
when they do not try to find joy in God
but in the things of this world.

FILL IN THE BLANKS

1. We must believe that God is .... (21)

2. God has shown his love for us because he said he would ....; because he saved us from ....; because he .... each one of us and .... like a father. (22)

3. When we think of God's love for us we should .... and we should .... (23)

4. We worship God by .... through Jesus in ....; by .... to God; by ....; by .... to honor him. (24)

5. We worship God especially in .... because in Holy Mass Jesus ...., as he did on the ...., but he does not suffer any more. He gives God .... (25)

6. We do God's will by .... and by doing everything we can to .... (26)

7. We use God's gifts to honor him when we ...., and when we .... to give him honor. (27)

8. We should hope and pray for the help we need to .... and to be .... (28)

9. God put us in this world to .... and .... him, to .... him by doing his .... to get ourselves ready for .... (29)

10. People show that they do not love God when they
    do not .... him; when they do not ....
    in prayer; when they do not .... but in the
    thing of .... (30)

CAN YOU ANSWER THESE?

1. What do we know about God? (21)

2. How do we know that God loves us? (22)

3. What do we owe God? (23)

4. How do we give worship to God? (24)

5. Why do we honor God most at Mass? (25)

6. How do we prove that we love God? (26)

7. How do we honor God? (27)

8. What should we especially pray for? (28)

9. What is our main duty in this world? (29)

10. How can we tell that we do not really love God? (30)

JESUS IS FOUND IN THE TEMPLE

WHEN Jesus was a boy, twelve years old, he
he was taken up to the feast of the Passover.
For the first time he saw the holy city of Jerusalem
and the Temple of the Lord. He knew he was in
his Father's house.

The boy Jesus was so filled with love for his Father and the worship of the Temple that when it was time to go home to Nazareth, he stayed behind. The group of people who were traveling together was large, and at first he was not missed. But when night came and Jesus could not be found, his mother became very worried. The next day Mary and Joseph left their group and hurried back to Jerusalem. They could not find him.

On the third day, they went up to the Temple. There they found Jesus, sitting with the teachers of the law, listening to their words and asking them questions. Everyone was surprised at this boy's knowledge of the word of God.

His mother spoke to him sadly, "Son, why have you done this to us? Your father and I have been searching for you in sorrow."

"Why did you search for me?" said Jesus. "Did you not know I had to be in my Father's house?"

Jesus went back to Nazareth with them then and was obedient to them. His mother kept all these things in her heart for Jesus reminded her that we are in this world to know and love God, and to serve him by doing his will.

Part Two — CREATION

Chapter **The Beginning**
3 **of the**
History of Salvation

31. What do we mean when we say that God is the Creator?

When we say that God is the Creator
we mean that he made all things
from nothing.

32. What is the beginning of the mystery of salvation?

The creation of angels and the world
is the beginning
of the mystery of salvation.

33. Which are the chief creatures of God?
The chief creatures of God are
angels and men.

34. What are angels?
Angels are spirits without bodies.

35. Who are the good angels?
The good angels obeyed God
and are now in heaven
  with him.
They help us to be good.

36. Who are the bad angels?
The bad angels disobeyed God
and are now called devils,
who tempt us to sin.

37. What is the first gift of God leading to Christ?
The creation of man
is the first gift of God leading to Christ.

38. What is man?
Man is a creature with a body and a soul,
made to the image of God.

39. Why is man made to the image of God?
Man is made to the image of God
because, he has a soul, and, like God,
he can know and love.

40. Who were the first man and woman?
The first man and woman were
Adam and Eve.

41. How does God's work of saving us show itself?
God's work of saving us
began with the creation,
and showed itself in the life
of Jesus Christ on earth,
his death and resurrection.

42. How was God present among people?
God was present with the people of Israel.
He was present especially in the life,
death, and resurrection of his Son.

43. How is God present among us today?
God is present among us today,
showing his power and love to help us.

44. Can we come to know God through the things he created?
The Bible tells us
that we can come to know God
through the things he created,
as the beginning and end of all things.

45. How can we help people to find God?
We can help people to find God
by a life of faith in God
and a love of Jesus Christ.

FILL IN THE BLANKS

1. When we say that God is the Creator we mean
   .... (31)

2. The chief creatures of God are .... and
   .... (33)

3. Angels are .... made by God, without
   .... (34)

4. The good angels .... God and are now
   in .... They help us .... (35)

5. The bad angels .... God and are now
   called .... who tempt us to .... (36)

6. The first gift of God leading to Christ is ...... (37)

7. Man is a .... with a .... and a
   ...., made to the .... (38)

8. Man is made to the image of God because he has
   .... and, like God, he can ....
   and .... (39)

9. The first man and woman were .... (40)

10. God's work of saving us began with .... and
    showed itself in the .... on earth, his ......
    and .... (41)

11. God was present with .... He was present especially .... in his Son (42)

12. God is present among us today, showing his .... and to help us (43)

13. The Bible tells us that we can come to know God through .... as the .... and .... of all things (44)

14. We can help people to find God by .... and a .... of Jesus Christ. (45)

CAN YOU ANSWER THESE?

1. What has God created? (31)
2. What is the difference between angels and men? (34)
3. What do angels do for us? (35)
4. How do devils harm us? (36)
5. What does every person have? (38)
6. How is man like God? (39)
7. How did God show that he wanted to save us? (41)
8. Does God show that he is with us today? (43)
9. How can we come to know God? (44)
10. What should we do to help people to find God? (45)

THE STORY OF CREATION

GOD is eternal. He had no beginning, and he will have no end. God made the angels. They are spirits like the soul of man.

To have a beautiful place for man to live, God made the universe.

On the **first** day God made earth out of nothing. Then he said, "Let light be made," and at once light appeared. God separated light from darkness and called them day and night.

On the **second** day God made the blue sky.

On the **third** day God said, "Let the waters under heaven be gathered together into one place, and let the dry land appear. Let this dry land bring forth grass and trees and plants of every kind."

On the **fourth** day God made the sun, the moon, and the stars.

On the **fifth** day God made the fishes and other creatures that were to live in the water. He also made birds and other creatures that were to fly in the sky.

On the **sixth** day God made all the animals that were to live on the ground. Then God said, "I shall make man in my image. I shall make man to rule over all the things that I have created." God formed man out of the dust of the earth. Then he breathed into him a soul that will never die.

On the **seventh** day God rested from his work. He blessed that day and made it holy.

Chapter **4**

Jesus Christ, Savior and Redeemer of the World

46. What does the incarnation mean?

The incarnation means
that Jesus Christ,
the Son of God,
the second person of
the Blessed Trinity,
became man
and came
to live among us.

47. Why did the Son of God become man?

The Son of God became man
to bring us his own divine life
and to save us from sin.

48. How does Jesus Christ give us his divine life?

Jesus Christ gives us his divine life
through his sanctifying grace,
which makes us holy.

49. Where do we receive the new life of grace?

We receive the new life of grace in baptism
because in Christ we are made new persons
and God's children.

50. Why is Jesus called our Savior?

Jesus is called our Savior
because he saved us from the slavery of sin
and there is no salvation for anyone
without him.

51. Why is Jesus called our Redeemer?

Jesus is our Redeemer
because he paid our debt for sin
and bought heaven back for us
by his suffering and death on the cross,
and by his resurrection from the dead.

52. Why did Jesus die on the cross?

Jesus died on the cross
because it was his Father's will to save us
from the power of the devil and sin
and to lead us to heaven;
because Jesus loved us so much
that he was willing to give his life for us.

53. How was Jesus Christ made known to us as God's Son?

Jesus was made known to us
as God's Son in power
through his glorious resurrection,
for he was obedient even to death
and was raised up as Lord of all.

54. What has Jesus done for us through his resurrection?

Through his resurrection
Jesus gave eternal life to all,
and in him we are made new persons.

55. How was God present in the history of men?

God was present
in the history of the people of Israel;
he was at work especially
in the life, death and resurrection of his Son.

56. **How do we see God's love for us in the life of Jesus?**

We see God's love for us in the life of Jesus
because Jesus lived among people,
and reached out to help all—
the poor, the sick, and sinners.
He joined himself to everyone except in sin.

57. **How does the Risen Lord now help us?**

The Risen Lord teaches us
by his Word of Life in the Gospel;
he gives us the divine life of grace,
especially through the sacraments;
he gives us his Holy Spirit to make us holy
and pleasing to his Father.

58. What is God's plan for us?

God wants to lead us to eternal life with him
by making us his people
in union with his Son, Jesus Christ.

59. How does Jesus lead us to eternal life?

Jesus leads us to eternal life
especially through the Church he founded.

FILL IN THE BLANKS

1. The incarnation means that Jesus Christ, the Son
   of ...., the .... person of the
   Blessed Trinity, became .... and came
   to .... (46)

2. The Son of God became man to .... and
   to .... from sin. (47)

3. Jesus Christ gives us his divine life through ....
   .... (48)

4. We receive the new life of grace in ....
   because in Christ we are made ....
   and .... (49)

5. Jesus is called our Savior because ....
   from the slavery of .... and there is no
   salvation for anyone .... (50)

6. Jesus is our Redeemer because .... and
   .... by his .... and ....
   on the cross, and by his .... (51)

7. Jesus died on the cross because ....
   to save us from .... and ....
   and to lead us to ....; because Jesus
   .... that he was willing to give...........
   for us. (52)

8. Jesus was made known to us as God's Son in power
   through his .... for he was ....
   even to death and was .... as Lord
   of all. (53)

9. Through his .... Jesus gave eternal life
   to all, and in him we are made .... (54)

10. God was present in the history of the people of
    ....; he was at work especially in the
    ...., ... and .... of his
    Son. (55)

11. We see God's love for men in the life of Jesus
    because Jesus ...., and reached out to
    .... the poor, the ...., ...
    and the .... He joined himself to every-
    one except in .... (56)

12. The Risen Lord teaches us by his Word of Life in
    .... he gives us the divine life of grace,
    especially through ....; he gives us his
    Holy Spirit to .... and pleasing to
    .... (57)

13. God wants to lead us to .... by making us
    .... in union with .... (58)

14. Jesus leads us to .... especially through
    .... which he founded. (59)

CAN YOU ANSWER THESE?

1. Who became man for us? (46)
2. How did Jesus show his love for us? (48)
3. How are we made new men and God's children? (49)
4. From what did Jesus save us? (50)
5. How did Jesus redeem us? (51)
6. How did Jesus die for us? (52)
7. How did Jesus show that he was the Son of God? (53)
8. How does Jesus give eternal life to all? (54)
9. How was God at work among people? (55)
10. How does God show his love in the life of Jesus? (56)
11. How does Jesus help us now? (57)
12. How can we gain eternal life? (58)
13. How does Jesus lead us to eternal life? (59)

1 THE BIRTH OF JESUS CHRIST

JESUS Christ is God made man. He is God because he is the only Son of God, having the same divine nature as his Father. He is man because he is the Son of the Blessed Virgin Mary

and has a body and soul like ours. Yet Jesus is only one Person, the second Person of the Blessed Trinity.

Jesus became man and was born of the Virgin Mary so that he might suffer for us and teach us how to save our soul.

Mary and Joseph had to go to the town of Bethlehem. There was no room for them anywhere, so her Child was born in a stable.

Angels told some shepherds, and they went to see the Child. The Little Boy they saw was Jesus, the Son of God made man.

Three kings came from the East and brought him gifts. They adored him as the King of heaven and earth.

2   JESUS DIES ON THE CROSS

THE chief priests of the Jews and their servants brought Jesus to Pilate, the Roman Governor, that he might be condemned to death. After Pilate had him beaten with whips and crowned with thorns, he turned him over to the to the Roman soldiers who led Jesus out of the city of Jerusalem to the place of death called Calvary.

On Calvary the soldiers stripped Jesus and nailed him to the Cross. Standing by the Cross were his Mother, John the beloved disciple, Mary Magdalene and some of his friends.

After three hours of terrible pain on the Cross, Jesus said, "It is finished! Father, into your hands I commend my spirit." And Jesus died. God died that we sinners might live!

Later Nicodemus and Joseph, who were friends of Jesus, came to bury him. They placed the body of Jesus in Joseph's own new tomb, dug out of rock, in a garden near the place where the cross stood.

3 THE RESURRECTION OF JESUS

WHEN the apostles heard that their Master was dead, they returned to the house where they had eaten the Last Supper with him. They were very sad.

But on Sunday morning Jesus rose by his own divine power, a glorious Victor, as he had promised. The earth quaked as he came forth from the tomb, and the guards trembled with fear. His body shone like the sun. Death was conquered.

The Resurrection of Jesus is the strongest proof that Jesus is God. The whole truth and meaning of our faith rests upon this greatest of all his miracles.

By his suffering and Resurrection Jesus saved us from sin and opened heaven to us. He will raise us up and we shall be with him forever.

The Risen Jesus worships God in Holy Mass. We can worship God in union with him in the Mass. We can give God praise and thanksgiving, make up for our sins, and receive the grace we need to carry out God's will for us.

4 THE ASCENSION OF JESUS INTO HEAVEN

FORTY days after the Resurrection, five hundred followers of Jesus met on a mountain in Galilee. Jesus showed himself to them.

He said, "All authority in heaven and on earth has been given to me. Go, therefore, make disciples of all the nations; baptize them in the Name of the Father, and of the Son and of the Holy Spirit, and teach them to observe all the commands I gave you. And know that I am with you always; yes, to the end of time."

When they reached the Mount of Olives, Jesus said to the disciples, "Now I hand over to you the command of my Father. Stay in the city, then, until you are clothed with power from on high. You will receive power when the Holy Spirit comes upon you, and you are to be my witnesses in Jerusalem, throughout Judea and Samaria—yes, even to the ends of the earth."

Then while Jesus was blessing them, he began to rise in the air and was taken from their sight.

While the Apostles were still looking up into the sky, two angels dressed in white came to them. "Men of Galilee," they said, "why do you stand here looking at the sky? This Jesus who has been taken away from you up to heaven will come back in the same way that you saw him go."

The disciples returned to Jerusalem. They remained there, praising God and praying for the coming of the Holy Spirit.

Chapter 5 The Holy Spirit in the Church

60. Who is the Holy Spirit?

The Holy Spirit is God,
the third Person of the Holy Trinity.

61. What did Jesus tell us about the Holy Spirit?

Jesus told us that the Holy Spirit is God
and that he would send him from the Father
that he might remain with us.

62. When did the Holy Spirit come to the Church?

The Holy Spirit came at Pentecost,
fifty days after the resurrection of Jesus.

63. Where is the Holy Spirit present in a special way?

The Holy Spirit is present in a special way in the Church,
the community of people who believe in Christ as Lord.

64. What happens when a person accepts the Spirit of Christ?

When a person accepts the Spirit of Christ, God leads him to a new way of life.

FILL IN THE BLANKS

1. The Holy Spirit is . . . ., the . . . . Person of the Holy Trinity. (60)

2. Jesus told us that the Holy Spirit is . . . . and that he would . . . . that he might. . . . . (61)

3. The Holy Spirit came at . . . ., ... days after the resurrection of Jesus. (62)

4. The Holy Spirit is present in a special way . . . ., the community of people who . . . . Christ as Lord. (63)

5. When a person accepts the Spirit of Christ, God . . . . (64)

CAN YOU ANSWER THESE?

1. How do we know that the Holy Spirit is God? (61)

2. What happened on Pentecost? (62)

3. Is the Holy Spirit in the Catholic Church? (63)

4. How does God lead us to a new way of life? (64)

THE SENDING OF THE HOLY SPIRIT

TEN days after Jesus went to heaven, he sent the Holy Spirit to his Church.

When the Apostles were all together in the upper room in Jerusalem, the Mother of Jesus and the holy women being with them, they suddenly heard a sound from the sky like a mighty rushing wind. It seemed to fill the room where they were. And upon the head of each Apostle there appeared something that looked like a little flame of fire. They were all filled with the Holy Spirit.

People in Jerusalem heard the strange sound and came running. It was nine o'clock in the morning, but a crowd of people soon gathered around the Apostles, wondering what had happened.

The Apostles felt that a wonderful change had come over them. They were aware of new strength and power, for the Holy Spirit had come,

according to the promise of Jesus. Now the Apostles were able to speak in languages they had not known before.

In the crowd there were people from more than a dozen different lands. Each of them heard the Apostles talking in his own language.

Peter said to the people, "Be sorry for your sins, and be baptized in the Name of Jesus Christ. God will forgive you, and will give you the Holy Spirit. Save yourselves!"

On that day about three thousand souls were added to the number of disciples. They joined in the breaking of bread, and in prayer.

Chapter

6 The Catholic Church

65. What is the Church?

The Church is the new People of God,
prepared for in the Old Testament,
and given life, growth, and guidance
by Jesus Christ
in the Holy Spirit.

66. What are the gifts of God in the Catholic Church?

The gifts of God in the Catholic Church are:
the truths of faith,
and the sacraments.

67. Why did Jesus start the Church?

Jesus started the Church
to bring all men to eternal salvation.

68. What power did Jesus give to his apostles?

Jesus gave his apostles, the first bishops,
the power to teach
and to guide people to God
and to help them to be holy.

The Shepherds of God's people.

69. To whom did Jesus give special power in his Church?

Jesus gave special power in his Church
to Saint Peter
by making him the head of the apostles
and the chief teacher and ruler
of the Church.

70. Who takes our Lord's place today as head of the Church?

The Pope, the Bishop of Rome
takes our Lord's place
as head of the Church.

71. Who are the successors of the apostles?

The successors of the apostles,
who take their place
as shepherds of the Church, are the bishops.

72. Who help the bishops in the care of people?

The priests help the bishops
in the care of people.

73. What do we owe the Pope, bishops and priests?

We owe the Pope, bishops, and priests
love, respect, and obedience.

The New People of God

74. Who guides the Church and gives it life?

Jesus guides the Church and gives it
his own life of grace through the Holy Spirit,
whom he sent to his Church.

75. What do we believe about the Catholic Church?

We believe that the Catholic Church
is the ordinary means of salvation
in the world.

76. Why does Jesus want all who believe in him to be one?

Jesus wants all who believe in him to be one
so that the world may know
that he was sent by the Father
as the Savior and Redeemer of the world.

77. What mission did Jesus give to his Church?

Jesus gave his Church the mission
of bringing the message of salvation
to all men.

FILL IN THE BLANKS

1. The Church is the ...., prepared for
   in the ...., and given ...., ...
   and .... by .... in the .... (65)

2. The gifts of God in the Catholic Church are: ......
   ...., and the .... (66)

3. Jesus started the Church to .... (67)

4. Jesus gave his apostles, the first bishops, the power to .... and .... people to God and to .... (68)

5. Jesus gave special power in his Church to Saint Peter by .... and the .... and .... (69)

6. The Pope, the Bishop of Rome, takes .... place as .... (70)

7. The successors of the apostles, who take their place ...., are the .... (71)

8. The priests help .... in the care of people. (72)

9. We owe the Pope, bishops and priests, ..., ... and .... (73)

10. Jesus .... the Church and give is .... through .... whom he sent to his Church. (74)

11. We believe that the Catholic Church is .... of salvation in the world. (75)

12. Jesus wants all who believe in him to be one so that .... as the .... and .... of the world. (76)

13. Jesus gave his Church the mission of .... to all men. (77)

CAN YOU ANSWER THESE?

1. What does Jesus give to his Church? (66)
2. What does the Church do for us? (67)
3. What power did Jesus give his Apostles? (68)
4. What special power did Jesus give St. Peter? (69)
5. Who is the chief teacher and ruler of the Church? (70)
6. What is the work of the bishops? (71)
7. What is the work of priests? (72)
8. How does Jesus guide the Church and give it life? (74)
9. How does the Holy Spirit help the world? (75)
10. Why must the believers in Jesus be united? (76)
11. What is the mission of the Church in the world?

JESUS CALMS THE STORM

THE Apostles took Jesus into a boat and began to row across the lake. Jesus fell asleep.

When they were half way across, a great wind blew down from between the hills that were around the lake. The storm drove great waves of water into the boat, so that it was in danger of sinking. The apostles were afraid. They awoke Jesus, saying, "Lord, save us!"

Jesus stood up and looked out upon the sea. Then he said to the waves, "Peace, be still!"

At once the wind stopped blowing, the waves were quiet, and there was a great calm.

Jesus gave us the Catholic Church to be a sure and true guide to heaven, just as Jesus helped the apostles in the boat. He protected them and brought peace by calming them storm.

Jesus made Saint Peter the head of his Church on earth. The Pope is the head of the Church today. He takes the place of Jesus on earth. All the bishops are the followers of the apostles.

The Seven Sacraments — Sources of Grace

Chapter 7 — The Sacraments

78. How is the work of Jesus continued in the Church?

The work of Jesus is continued in the Church through the gift of the Holy Spirit.

79. How does the Holy Spirit act in the Church?

The Holy Spirit acts in the Church
especially in the sacraments
which Christ began.

80. What is a sacrament?

A sacrament is a sign that we can see,
which lets us know
that Jesus is giving his grace to the soul
of the person who receives the sacrament.

81. Why are the sacraments called actions of Christ?

The sacraments are called actions of Christ
because through them
he gives his Spirit to us
and makes us a holy people.

82. Why did Jesus give us the sacraments?

Jesus gave us the sacraments
to make us holy by his grace,
to build up his Church,
and to give worship to God.

83. Does the Church want us to receive the sacraments?

The Church wants us
to receive the sacraments often
and with faith
that we may receive the grace we need
to live a better Christian life.

FILL IN THE BLANKS

1. The work of Jesus is continued in the Church through .... (78)

2. The Holy Spirit acts in the Church especially in .... (79)

3. A sacrament is .... that we can ...., which lets us know that Jesus is .... to the soul of the person who .... (80)

4. The sacraments are called actions of Christ because through them .... and .... (81)

5. Jesus gave us the sacraments to ...., to .... and to .... (82)

6. The Church wants us to receive the sacraments .... and with .... that we may receive .... to live a .... (83)

CAN YOU ANSWER THESE?

1. What does the Holy Spirit do in the Church? (79)
2. How does Jesus give us his grace? (80)
3. How does Jesus give his Spirit to us? (81)
4. What does Jesus do for us in the sacraments? (82)
5. Why should we receive the sacraments often? (83)

SACRAMENT
OF
BAPTISM

84. What is baptism?

Baptism is a new birth as a child of God,
the beginning of a new life of God's grace
in us.

85. What does Jesus do for us in baptism?

Jesus himself baptizes and makes us holy
with the gifts of the Holy Spirit
and marks our soul
with a sign that cannot be taken away.
Jesus also welcomes us into his Church.

86. Does baptism take away sin?

Baptism takes away original sin,
the sin we received from our first parents,
and also any other sin.

FILL IN THE BLANKS

1. Baptism is a .... as a child of God, the beginning of God's grace in us. (84)

2. Jesus himself baptizes and makes us holy with .... and marks our soul with .... Jesus also .... into his Church. (85)

3. Baptism takes away ...., the sin we received from ...., and also .... sin. (86)

CAN YOU ANSWER THESE?

1. How can we become children of God? (84)
2. What kind of life do we receive from God at baptism? (84)
3. Who really baptizes us? (85)
4. How does Jesus make us holy in baptism? (85)
5. When do we become members of the Catholic Church? (85)
6. What sins does baptism take away? (86)

**SACRAMENT
OF
CONFIRMATION**

87. What is confirmation?

Confirmation is the sacrament
by which those born again in baptism
now receive again the Holy Spirit,
the gift of the Father and the Son.

88. What does Jesus do for us in confirmation?

In confirmation Jesus sends
the Holy Spirit to us again
and gives us new strength
to live a Christian life.

89. What duty do we have after we are confirmed?

After confirmation we have the duty
to bring Jesus Christ, his example,
and his Church to others
and to serve our fellow men.

90. Who helps us to be a witness to Jesus Christ?

By the strength of his grace
the Holy Spirit helps us
to be a witness to Jesus Christ.

FILL IN THE BLANKS

1. Confirmation is the sacrament by which those born again in baptism now ...., the gift of .... (87)

2. In confirmation Jesus sends .... and gives us .... to lead .... (88)

3. After confirmation we have the duty to .... and to serve .... (89)

4. By the strength of his grace the Holy Spirit .... to be a .... (90)

CAN YOU ANSWER THESE?

1. How do we receive the Holy Spirit? (87)
2. Who is the Holy Spirit? (87)
3. Why does Jesus send us the Holy Spirit? (88)
4. What must we do after Confirmation? (89)
5. How does the Holy Spirit help us to be a witness to Jesus? (90)

**SACRAMENT
OF
PENANCE**

91. What is penance?

Penance is the sacrament
which brings us God's forgiveness
for the sins we committed after baptism.

92. What does Jesus do for us in penance?

In penance Jesus comes to forgive our sins
and brings peace with God
and with the Church,
which is hurt by our sins.

93. How does Jesus help us to be holy in penance?

In penance Jesus sends his Holy Spirit
to our soul with grace and strength
to live a better Christian life
and to keep away from sin.

94. Why must we be sorry for our sins before they can be forgiven?

We must be sorry
for our sins
before they can be
  forgiven
because by our sins
we have offended God,
our Father,
and because Jesus
suffered on the cross
for our sins.

95. What does true sorrow for sin do for us?

True sorrow for sin
brings back the grace
of God if we have lost it
by serious (mortal) sin.

96. What must we do if we have committed a serious sin?

If we have committed a serious sin
we must receive the sacrament of penance
before receiving the Holy Eucharist.

97. Why does the Church want us to receive the sacrament of penance often?

The Church wants us
to receive the sacrament of penance often,
even if we do not have any serious sin,
because we need the help of Jesus
to keep away from sin
and to live a holy life.

FILL IN THE BLANKS

1. Penance is the sacrament which brings us ......
...... for the sins we committed after ....
(91)

2. In penance Jesus comes to .... and brings
.... which is hurt by our sins. (92)

3. In penance Jesus sends .... to our soul
with .... and .... to live a better
.... and to .... (93)

4. We must be sorry for our sins before they can be forgiven because by our sins ...., and because .... (94)

5. True sorrow for sins brings back .... if we have lost it by .... (95)

6. If we have committed a serious sin we must .... before receiving the Holy Eucharist. (96)

7. The Church wants us to receive the sacrament of penance often, even if we do not have any serious sin, because .... to keep away from .... and to live .... (97)

CAN YOU ANSWER THESE?

1. How do we get God's forgiveness? (91)

2. How do we hurt the Church? (92)

3. What does Jesus do for us in the sacrament of penance? (93)

4. What have our sins done to our heavenly Father and to Jesus (94)

5. How do we get back the grace of God, if we lost it by serious sin? (95)

6. If we have committed a mortal sin, can we receive Holy Communion? (96)

7. Why should we receive the sacrament of penance often? (97)

8. How do you make an act of contrition? (Essential Prayers — p. 121.)

SACRAMENT
OF
HOLY ORDERS

98. What is Holy Orders?

Holy Orders is the sacrament
by which Jesus shares
the work of his priesthood with other men—
the bishops and priests
of the Catholic Church.

99. What does Jesus do through his priests?

Through his priests
Jesus makes himself present
to offer the Sacrifice of the Mass,
to baptize,
to give the sacrament of confirmation,
to give his body and blood in Communion,
to forgive sins in the sacrament of penance,
to anoint the sick and to bless marriages.

100. What special graces does Jesus give in Holy Orders?

Through Holy Orders Jesus gives
the special grace of the Holy Spirit
to guide and take care of those
who believe in him,
to teach and preach his gospel,
and to help God's People
to live a better Christian life.

FILL IN THE BLANKS

1. Holy Orders is the sacrament by which Jesus . . . .
. . . . with other men—the . . . . and
. . . . of the Catholic Church. (98)

2. Through his priests Jesus makes himself present
to . . . . of the Mass, to . . . .; to
give the sacrament of . . . ., to give . . . .
in Communion, to forgive sins in . . . .,
to anoint the . . . . and to bless . . . .
(99)

3. Through Holy Orders Jesus gives the special grace
of the Holy Spirit to . . . . and . . . .
those who believe in him, to . . . . and
. . . . the gospel, and to . . . . God's
people to . . . . Christian life. (100)

CAN YOU ANSWER THESE?

1. Who shares the priesthood of Jesus Christ? (98)
2. What does Jesus do for us through his priests? (99)
3. Why does Jesus give special grace of the Holy Spirit to priests? (100)

**SACRAMENT
OF THE
ANOINTING
OF THE SICK**

101. What is the Anointing of the Sick?

The Anointing of the Sick is the sacrament for the seriously ill, infirm, and aged.

102. What does Jesus do for the sick in this sacrament?

Jesus comes to the sick in this sacrament
to bring health to the sick persons,
to lighten their suffering,
to forgive their sins,
and to bring them to eternal life with God.

FILL IN THE BLANKS

1. The Anointing of the Sick is the sacrament for

   ...., ... and .... (101)

2. Jesus comes to the sick in this sacrament to ....

   .... to sick persons, to .... their

   sufferings, to .... their sins, and to bring

   them to .... (102)

CAN YOU ANSWER THESE?

1. Who receives the Anointing of the Sick? (101)

2. Why do the sick receive the sacrament of the
   Anointing? (102)

SACRAMENT
OF
MATRIMONY

103. What is matrimony?

Matrimony is a sacrament
in which Jesus Christ makes marriage
a lifelong, sacred union of husband and wife,
by which they give themselves to each other
and to him.

104. What does Jesus do for the married?

Jesus comes to man and wife
to give them his grace
to help them to do their duty to God,
to each other, and to their children.

FILL IN THE BLANKS

1. Matrimony is a sacrament in which Jesus Christ
   .... of husband and wife, by which they
   give themselves to .... and to .... (103)

2. Jesus comes to man and wife to .... to
   help them to do ...., to ...., and
   to .... (104)

CAN YOU ANSWER THESE?

1. What does Jesus do in the Sacrament of Matrimony?
   (103)

2. How long does mariage last? (103)

3. What should children do for their parents? (104)

LAZARUS IS RAISED FROM THE DEAD

MARTHA and Mary were friends of Jesus. When their brother Lazarus died, they sent for Jesus. As he came near, Martha ran out to meet him and said, "Master, if you had been here, my brother would not have died."

Jesus said, "Your brother will rise again. I am the resurrection and the life. He who believes in me will live even if he dies."

"Do you believe this?" Jesus asked.

"Yes, Lord," she replied. "I have come to believe that you are the Messiah, the Son of God: he who is to come into the world."

Mary came and bowed in sorrow at the feet of Jesus. And seeing her tears and the sadness of her friends who stood nearby, Jesus wept.

As he came to the tomb, the men moved away the stone from the entrance of the cave. And Jesus turned to God in prayer.

Jesus looked upward and said: "Father, I thank you for having heard me. I know that you always hear me but I have said this for the sake of the crowd, that they may believe that you sent me."

Then he called with a loud voice, "Lazarus, come out!" And he who had been dead came out alive. Many of the Jews then believed in Jesus.

This miracle of the raising of Lazarus from the dead reminds us that Jesus will raise our bodies from the grave at the Last Judgment.

It also reminds us that Jesus is our resurrection and our life through the seven Sacraments which he has given to his Church. Through them the divine life of grace is given to our souls. But we must have faith in Jesus, who helps us through his sacraments.

Chapter
8

Sacrament
of the
Holy Eucharist

— HOLY MASS —

105. What is the Holy Eucharist?

The Holy Eucharist is the sacrament
in which Christ himself,
true God and true Man,
is really present,
offered, and received
in a mysterious way,
under the appearances of bread and wine.

106. What do we mean by the appearances of bread and wine?

By the appearances of bread and wine
we mean the things
that we can see, touch, and taste—
color, taste, weight, and shape.

73

107. When did Jesus give us the Holy Eucharist?

Jesus gave us the Holy Eucharist
at the Last Supper,
the night before he died.

108. What happened at the Last Supper?

At the Last Supper,
when Jesus said, "This is my body,"
the bread was changed into his body;
and when he said, "This is my blood,"
the wine was changed into his blood.

109. When did Jesus give his priests the power to change bread and wine into his body and blood?

Jesus gave his priests the power
to change bread and wine
into his body and blood
when he said to the apostles
at the Last Supper:
"Do this in memory of me."

110. What happens when a priest speaks the words of consecration at Holy Mass?

When a priest speaks
the words of consecration at Holy Mass,
the bread and wine is changed
into the body and blood of Christ,
given in sacrifice.

111. How is Jesus given in sacrifice at Holy Mass?

Jesus is given in sacrifice at Holy Mass
because the Mass not only reminds us
of the sacrifice of the cross on Calvary,
but because Jesus really gives himself
to his heavenly Father,
as he did on the cross,
but now in an unbloody manner
in this sacrament,
for he cannot suffer anymore.

112. Why does Jesus give himself to his Father in the Mass?

Jesus gives himself to his Father in the Mass
to continue for all time the sacrifice of the cross
until he will come again,
to adore and thank his Father,
to ask pardon for our sins
and to bring his blessing upon us.

THE LAST SUPPER

AT THE supper Jesus took a piece of bread, blessed it, and broke it. Then he gave it to the apostles and said, "Take and eat; this is my Body."

Then he took a cup with wine in it, blessed it in the same way and said, "All of you drink of this; for this is my Blood of the new covenant, which is being shed for many for the forgiveness of sins. Do this in memory of me."

Our Lord changed bread and wine into his Body and Blood and offered himself to God. This was an unbloody sacrifice. At the same time he told the apostles that he would die on the next day. This would be the bloody sacrifice.

But Jesus wanted this unbloody sacrifice to continue on earth till the end of time. When he told the apostles to do as he had done, he made them priests who could offer this sacrifice. They could pass this power on to other priests in the future.

FILL IN THE BLANKS

1. The Holy Eucharist is the sacrament in which ...., true .... and true ...., is really ...., ..., and .... in a mysterious way, under the appearances of .... and .... (105)

2. By the appearances of .... and .... we mean the things we can ...., ... and .... color, ..., weight, and .... (106)

3. Jesus gave us the Holy Eucharist at ...., the night before he .... (107)

4. At the Last Supper, when Jesus said, "This is ....," the .... was changed into his ....; and when he said, "This is ....," the .... was changed into his ...... (108)

5. Jesus gave his priests the power to .... **into** his .... when he said to the apostles **at the** Last Supper: "Do this ...." (109)

6. When a priest speaks the words .... at Holy Mass, the ....and .... is changed into the .... and .... of Christ, given in .... (110)

7. Jesus is given .... at Holy Mass because the Mass not only .... us of the sacrifice of .... on Calvary, but because Jesus really .... to his heavenly Father, as he did on ...., but now in an .... manner in this sacrament for he cannot .... anymore. (111)

8. Jesus gives himself to his Father in the Mass to .... for all time the .... until he will come again, to .... and .... his Father, to .... for our sins and to bring .... upon us. (112)

CAN YOU ANSWER THESE?

1. How is Jesus present in the Holy Eucharist? (105)
2. What is the Last Supper? (107)

3. What happened when Jesus said, "This is my body"? (108)

4. What happened when Jesus said, "This is my blood?" (108)

5. What power did Jesus give at the Last Supper? (109)

6. Why do priests have the power to change bread and wine into the body and blood of Jesus? (109)

7. When is the bread and wine changed into the body and blood of Christ? (110)

8. Why are we reminded of the death of Jesus at Holy Mass? (111)

9. What does Jesus do for his Father at Mass? (112)

10. What does Jesus do for us at Mass? (112)

— HOLY COMMUNION —

113. What is Holy Communion?

Holy Communion is a meal
of the body and blood of Jesus Christ
which reminds us of the Last Supper
and nourishes us with the life of God,
by giving us his grace.

114. What does Jesus do for us in the Eucharist?

In the Eucharist Jesus nourishes us
with his own self, the Bread of Life,

so that we may become
a people more pleasing to God
and filled with greater love of God
and our neighbor.

115. Why is the Eucharist a sacrament of unity?

The Eucharist is a sacrament of unity
because it unites us more closely
with God and with one another
in divine love.

116. What must we do to receive the Eucharist worthily?

To receive the Eucharist worthily
we must be in the state of grace,
not in a state of serious sin.

117. When must we go to confession before Holy Communion?

We must go to confession
before Holy Communion
when we are sure
that we committed a serious sin.

118. Why is the Eucharist kept in our churches?

The Eucharist is kept in our churches
so that we may adore, thank, and love Jesus
and ask for his help
for ourselves and others.

THE LOAVES AND FISHES

A GREAT crowd, over five thousand men, besides women and children, were listening to Jesus. Toward evening, some of the apostles asked Jesus to send the crowd away, for it was near their supper time.

But Jesus said, "You yourselves can give them some food." Knowing that they had enough food only for themselves, Andrew said, "A boy here has five loaves of bread and two fish. But what are they among so many people?"

Jesus had the people sit down on the grass. Then he took into his hands the five loaves and two fish. Looking up to heaven, Jesus thanked his Father and blessed the food. He then broke it and had the apostles give to the people as much as each one needed. After they had all eaten enough , twelve baskets were gathered of what remained.

This miracle is a picture of the Holy Eucharist. At Holy Mass, through his priest, Jesus feeds our souls with the Bread of Life—his body and blood, in Holy Communion.

FILL IN THE BLANKS

1. Holy Communion is . . . . of the . . . . and . . . . of Jesus Christ which reminds us of . . . . and nourishes us with . . . . (113)

2. In the Eucharist Jesus nourishes us with his . . . ., and Bread . . . ., so that we may become . . . . and filled with . . . . of God and neighbor. (114)

3. The Eucharist is a sacrament of unity because
.... with God and with one another in

divine .... (115)

4. To receive the Eucharist worthily we must ......
............, not in a state of .... (116)

5. We must go to confession before Holy Communion
when .... (117)

6. The Eucharist is kept in our churches so that we
may ...., and .... Jesus and
.... his help for .... and ....
(118)

CAN YOU ANSWER THESE?

1. Why is Holy Communion like a meal? (113)

2. What does Jesus do for us in Holy Communion?
(114)

3. Why does Holy Communion help us to love one
another? (115)

4. If we have committed a serious sin, what must we
do before going to Holy Communion? (117)

5. How can we show our love for Jesus in the Eucharist? (118)

Jesus gave Peter and the Apostles power to forgive sins.

Part Seven — SIN

Chapter
9 The Sins of Man

119. How did Adam and Eve sin?

Adam and Eve sinned
by disobeying a commandment of God,
because they listened to the Evil One.

120. What happened to us on account of the sin of Adam?

On account of the sin of Adam
we come into the world
without God's life of grace in us
and we are filled with selfishness.

121. What is this sin in us called?

This sin in us is called original sin.

122. What is personal sin?

Personal sin is committed by a person
who breaks a law of God
knowingly and willingly.

123. What happens when we commit a serious sin?

When we commit a serious sin
we fail in love of God,
and turn away from doing his will
by a serious offense.

124. What must we believe about God's forgiveness?

We must believe that God is merciful
and will pardon the sinner
who is truly sorry,
and by the power of his grace
will draw him to salvation.

FILL IN THE BLANKS

1. Adam and Eve sinned by .... of God, because they .... (119)

2. On account of the sin of Adam we come into the world without .... and we are filled with .... (120)

3. This sin in us is called .... (121)

4. Personal sin is committed by .... who breaks a law of God .... and .... (122)

5. When we commit a serious sin we .... of God, and .... doing his will be .... (123)

6. We must believe that God is merciful and will pardon the sinner who ...., and by the power of his grace will .... (124)

CAN YOU ANSWER THESE?

1. Why did Adam and Eve disobey God? (119)

2. What did original sin do to us? (120)

3. Who commits a personal sin? (122)

4. When do we commit a serious sin? (123)

5. Why is God merciful? (124)

A PARALYZED MAN IS CURED

JESUS was preaching in a house. There were so many people that some had to stay outside.

Four men came carrying a paralyzed man. They could not reach Jesus through the crowd. So they lifted the man up to the top of the house and opened the roof. Then they lowered the sick man into the house, right at the feet of Jesus.

Seeing their faith, Jesus said to the sick man, "My friend, your sins are forgiven you."

The scribes and the Pharisees said, "Who is this man who utters blasphemies? Who can forgive sins but God alone?"

Jesus knew their thoughts and answered by saying, "To make it clear to you that the Son of Man has authority on earth to forgive sins" —he then addressed the paralyzed man, " I say to you, get up! Take your mat with you, and return to your house."

At once the paralyzed man stood up, and walked out through the crowd, praising God.

Jesus told the people that he worked this miracle to show that he had the power to forgive sins because he was God.

Jesus offered his life on the cross to take away our sins and to obtain God's forgiveness for them. Through the power he has given to his Apostles and to those who would follow them, the bishops and priests, he forgives our sins in the sacrament of penance.

Part Eight — THE LIFE OF GRACE —

Chapter 10 The New Life in the Spirit

125. What happens when a person accepts the Spirit of Christ?

When a person accepts the Spirit of Christ, God leads him to a new way of life.

126. What does this new way of life do for us?

This new way of life
makes us share in God's own life
by faith, hope, and love.

127. What is faith?

Faith is a gift
by which the Holy Spirit helps us
to accept God's word
and to give ourselves to the Father.

128. What is hope?

Hope is a gift
which helps us to know that God loves us
and cares for us
and that we can trust in him.

129. What is love?

Love is a gift which helps us to love God
and to love all people for the love of God
because they too belong to him.

130. What is sanctifying grace?

Sanctifying grace
is a gift of God
by which our soul shares
in the very life of God.

131. What does grace do for us?

Through grace the Holy Spirit
makes us holy and pleasing to God
and helps us to live as children of God.

132. Is grace also God's gift of himself?

Grace is also God's gift of himself
because the Holy Spirit unites us with God
by love
and dwells in our soul as in a temple.

133. What has God willed for our salvation?

God has willed
that we receive sanctifying grace
as his children
and that we reach eternal life with him.

FILL IN THE BLANKS

1. When a person accepts the Spirit of Christ, God leads him to .... (125)

2. This new way of life makes us ...... by ...., ..., and .... (126)

3. Faith is a .... by which the Holy Spirit .... to accept .... and to give ourselves to .... (127)

4. Hope is a .... which helps us .... and .... and that we can .... (128)

5. Love is a gift which .... and to .... for the love of God because .... (129)

6. Sanctifying grace is .... by which our shares in .... (130)

7. Through grace the Holy Spirit .... and .... and .... as children of God. (131)

8. Grace is also God's gift of .... because the Holy Spirit unites us with .... and dwells in .... (132)

9. God has willed that we receive .... and that we .... with him. (133)

CAN YOU ANSWER THESE?

1. How does God lead us to a new way of life? (125)
2. How do we share God's own life? (126)
3. What does the Holy Spirit help us to do through faith? (127)
4. What does the Holy Spirit help us to do through hope? (128)
5. What does the Holy Spirit help us to do through love? (129)
6. How do we share the life of God? (130)
7. What does the Holy Spirit do for us through grace? (131)
8. Does the Holy Spirit dwell in us? (132)
9. How do we reach eternal life with God? (133)

THE SERMON ON THE MOUNT

ON the mountain Jesus started to preach to his disciples and to the great crowd of people who had gathered there. Jesus spoke of the kingdom of God and how men must live who become members of it.

"Blest are the poor in spirit: the reign of God is theirs.

"Blest are the sorrowing: they shall be consoled.

"Blest are the lowly: they shall inherit the land.

"Blest are they who hunger and thirst for holiness: they shall have their fill.

"Blest are they who show mercy; mercy shall be theirs.

"Blest are the single-hearted; for they shall see God.

"Blessed are the peacemakers; they shall be called sons of God.

"Blest are those persecuted for holiness' sake: the reign of God is theirs."

In these words Jesus spoke of the main virtues of the Christian life. They are called the Beatitudes. If we live according to the Beatitudes, we shall surely keep God's Commandments.

When we accept the teaching of Jesus, he leads us to a new way of life. We live in the state of sanctifying grace by which our soul shares in the very life of God. With the help of God's grace we can practice virtue and reach the happiness of heaven.

Chapter **Perfect Christian**
11 **Love**

134. What must we do to answer God's love for us?

To answer God's love for us
we must obey everything
that Jesus has commanded,
and believe all that he has taught.

95

135. **What is the greatest commandment of God?**

The greatest commandment of God
is to love him with all our heart
and all people for his sake.

136. **When are we truly holy?**

We are truly holy when we love God
with all our heart.

137. **When do we love God with all our heart?**

We love God with all our heart
when we do all that he wants us to do,
and try to please him in all things.

138. **Why should love of God be in everything we do?**

Love of God should be in everything we do
because God is love,
and his love comes to us
through Jesus Christ.

139. **What is the "new commandment" which Jesus gave us?**

The new commandment
which Jesus gave us is:
"Love one another as I have loved you."

140. How do we show our love for God?
We show our love for God
by keeping the Commandments
and the laws of the Church,
by following the teaching of Jesus
in the Gospel,
and by practising the virtues,
especially love of God and neighbor.

FILL IN THE BLANKS

1. To answer God's love for us we must ....
   that Jesus has ...., and ....
   that he has .... (134)

2. The greatest commandment of God is ....
   with all our heart and our .... for his
   sake. (135)

3. We are truly holy when we .... (136)

4. We love God with all our heart when we ....
   and .... in all things (137)

5. Love of God should be everything we do because
   God ...., and his love comes to us
   .... (138)

6. The new commandment which Jesus gave us is:
   "....................." (139)

7. We show our love for God by ....
   and ...., by .... in the
   Gospel, by .... the virtues, especially
   .... (140)

CAN YOU ANSWER THESE?

1. How do we show our love for God? (134)

2. What does God want us to do more than anything
   else? (135)

3. How do we show that we love God with all our heart?
   (137)

4. Why does God deserve our love? (138)

5. How must we love each other? (139)

6. What must we do if we want to love God with all
   our heart? (140)

JESUS TEACHES THE COMMANDMENT OF LOVE

WHEN Jesus was thirty years old he began to
teach the people. He told them what God
wanted them to do to please him and to get to
heaven.

Once a lawyer asked him, "Teacher, what
must I do to inherit everlasting life?" Jesus answered him: "What is written in the law? How
do you read it?"

He answered: "You shall love the Lord your
God with all your heart, with all your soul, with

all your strength, and with all your mind; and your neighbor as yourself."

"Jesus said, "You have answered correctly. Do this and you shall live."

The commandment of love of God and the neighbor is the greatest of all commandments. We are truly holy only when we love God with all our heart, and when we love our neighbor for his sake.

THE COMMANDMENTS ARE OUR WAY TO HEAVEN

The Commandments of God

141. What are our duties toward God?

Our duties toward God are:
to do his will first in our lives,
to act as children toward him,
our loving Father,
to offer him our worship and prayer.

142. What are our duties toward our fellow man?

Our duties toward our fellowman are:
to be kind to him
in our thoughts, words, and actions,
to try to help others wherever we can,
to obey those who have a right
to command us
at home, in the Church,
and in our government.

143. What are our duties toward ourself?

Our duties toward ourself are:
to be an example of Christian goodness,
to be humble and patient
with ourselves and others,
to be pure in words and actions.

144. What are we commanded by the first commandment of God?

The first commandment is:
I, the Lord, am your God.
You shall not have other gods besides me.
We must not put anyone or anything
in place of God.

145. What are we commanded by the second commandment?

The second commandment is:
You shall not take
the name of the Lord, your God, in vain.
We must always speak with reverence
of God and the saints.

146. What are we commanded by the third commandment?

The third commandment is:
Remember to keep holy the sabbath day.
We must worship God on Sunday
by assisting at the Holy Sacrifice
of the Mass.

147. What are we commanded by the fourth commandment?

The fourth commandment is:
Honor your father and your mother.
We must love and obey our parents.

148. What are we commanded by the fifth commandment?

The fifth commandment is:
You shall not kill.
We must take our care of our health
and help others to do the same.

149. What are we commanded by the sixth commandment?

The sixth commandment is:
You shall not commit adultery.
We must be pure in our words and actions.

150. What are we commanded by the seventh commandment?

The seventh commandment is:
You shall not steal.
We must respect what belongs to others.

151. What are we commanded by the eighth commandment?

The eighth comandment is:
You shall not bear false witness
against your neighbor.
We must speak the truth in all things.

152. What are we commanded by the ninth commandment?

The ninth commandment is:
You shall not covet your neighbor's wife.
We must be pure in thought and in desire.

153. What are we commanded by the tenth commandment?

The tenth commandment is:
You shall not covet
anything that belongs to your neighbor.
We must not want to take or to keep
what belongs to others.

FILL IN THE BLANKS

1. Our duties toward God are to ...., to
    ...., our loving Father, to ....
    our .... and .... (141)

2. Our duties toward our fellowman are: to be ......
    .... in our ...., ..., and
    ....; to try to .... when we can,
    to .... at ...., in the ....
    and in our .... (142)

3. Our duties toward our self are to be an example of
    ...., to be .... and ....
    with ourselves and others, to be ....
    in .... and .... (143)

4. The first commandment is: ....
    .... We must not ....
    in place of God. (144)

5. The second commandment is: ....
    .... We must always ....
    of God and the saints. (145)

6. The third commandment is: ....
    We must worship God on Sunday by ....
    (146)

7. The fourth commandment is: ....
    We must .... our parents. (147)

8. The fifth commandment is: ....
    We must take care of .... and ....
    (148)

9. The sixth commandment is: ....
   We must be .... (149)

10. The seventh commandment is: ....
    We must .... (150)

11. The eighth commandment is: ....
    We must .... (151)

12. The ninth commandment is: ....
    We must be .... (152)

13. The tenth commandment is: ....
    We must not want to .... (153)

CAN YOU ANSWER THESE?

1. What does God want us to do for him? (141)

2. What does God want us to do for our fellowman? (142)

3. What does God want us to do for ourselves? (143)

4. What does God ask us to do in the first commandment? (144)

5. What does God ask us to do in the second commandment? (145)

6. What does God ask us to do in the third commandment? (146)

7. What does God ask us to do in the fourth commandment? (147)

8. What does God ask us to do in the fifth commandment? (148)

9. What does God ask us to do in the sixth commandment? (149)

10. What does God ask us to do in the seventh commandment? (150)

11. What does God ask us to do in the eighth commandment? (151)

12. What does God ask us to do in the ninth commandment? (152)

13. What does God ask us to do in the tenth commandment? (153)

JESUS WELCOMES CHILDREN

SOME of the women who listened to Jesus wanted him to put his hands on the heads of their little children to bless them. The disciples saw the women coming, and they thought that Jesus was too busy to bother with little children.

But Jesus was displeased that the disciples were sending the children away, and said to them, "You must let little children come to me, and you must never stop them. The Kingdom of Heaven belongs to little children like these."

Then Jesus took the little children up in his arms and laid his hands on their heads and blessed them. The mothers went home happy.

The disciples came to Jesus with the question, "Who is really the greatest in the Kingdom of Heaven?"

Jesus called a little boy to his side and set him in the middle of them all. "Believe me," he said, "unless you change and become like little children you will never enter the Kingdom of Heaven. The one who makes himself as little as this little child is the greatest in the Kingdom of Heaven."

Chapter **13**

Mary
Mother of God and the Church

154. Why is Mary in the Church in a place highest after Christ?

Mary is in the Church
in a place highest after Christ
because she is the Mother of Jesus Christ,
our Lord and God,
and because she is our spiritual Mother.

155. What special gifts did Mary receive from God?

The special gifts Mary received from God
are these:
she is the Mother of God,
she was kept free from original sin,
she was taken body and soul to heaven.

156. How should we honor the Blessed Virgin Mary?

We should honor the Blessed Virgin Mary
by showing her our love and devotion
as the Mother of Christ,
the Mother of the Church,
and our spiritual Mother.

157. Why does the Church honor the other saints?

The Church honors the other saints
because they help us by their prayers
and by the good example of their lives.

158. What must we do for those who have died?

We must honor the bodies
of those who have died
and pray for their souls.

FILL IN THE BLANKS

1. Mary is in the Church in a place highest after Christ because she is ...., and because she is .... (154)

2. The special gifts Mary received from God are these: she is ...., she was kept free from ...., she was taken .... to heaven. (155)

3. We should honor the Blessed Virgin Mary .... as Mother of Christ, Mother of the ...., and our .... (156)

4. The Church honors the other saints because they .... and by the good example .... (157)

5. We must .... the bodies of those who have died and .... and their souls. (158)

CAN YOU ANSWER THESE?

1. Why do we honor the Blessed Virgin Mary in the Church? (154)

2. How did God show his love for the Blessed Virgin Mary? (155)

3. How can we show our love for the Blessed Virgin Mary? (156)

4. How can the saints help us? (157)

5. How can we help those who have died? (158)

THE ANGEL SPEAKS TO MARY

THE hour was at hand for which God had been preparing his people. Not only the Jews, but all the world was looking for a Redeemer. They prayed that God would now keep the promise he made to Adam and Eve and had repeated again and again through the prophets.

The Angel Gabriel was sent from God to a young girl named Mary, who was soon to be married to Joseph, a very good man who also lived in Nazareth.

**Mary becomes
the Mother
of God.**

Gabriel said to Mary, "Hail full of grace, the Lord is with you." Mary was troubled and wondered about this greeting.

The Angel continued, "Do not be afraid, Mary, for you have found grace with God. Behold, you shall conceive in your womb and shall bring forth a Son; and you shall call his name Jesus."

After learning that this was to be accomplished by the power of God, Mary did not hesitate, but said, "Behold the handmaid of the Lord; be it done to me according to your word."

As soon as Mary gave this answer, she became the Mother of God. The Second Person of the Blessed Trinity, the Son of God, took to himself a body and soul like ours. He became man and dwelt among us. This is called the mystery of the Incarnation.

Chapter **14**

Reunion with God

159. What should we look forward to during this life?

During this life we should look forward to our reunion with God.

160. What is the judgment passed on each one of us after death?

The judgment which will be passed on each one of us after death is called the particular judgment.

161. What rewards or punishments do men receive after the particular judgment?

The rewards and punishments men will receive after the particular judgment are heaven, purgatory, or hell.

162. What happens in purgatory?

In purgatory our soul is made clean
before we are able to see God.

163. What will Jesus do when he returns with power as Judge?

When Jesus returns with power as Judge
he will hand over his people to the Father.

164. What will we do on the day of the last judgment?

On the day of the last judgment
all of us will stand
before the judgment seat of Christ,
so that each one may receive
what he deserves,
according to what he has done on earth,
good or evil.

165. What will happen to those who have done evil and turned from God?

Those who have done evil
and turned from God
will rise from the dead
and will be damned in hell forever.

166. What will happen to those who have done good?

Those who have done good
will rise to live an eternal life with God
and will receive the reward
of seeing him in unending joy.

167. **What should we do during our life on earth?
earth?**

During our life on earth
we should love and serve God faithfully
so that we may be ready for our death
and our resurrection with Christ
to eternal life in heaven.

THE GRAVE

RESURRECTION OF THE BODY

FILL IN THE BLANKS

1. During this life we should look forward to ......
.... (159)

2. The judgment which will be passed on each one of
us after death is called .... (160)

3. The rewards or punishments men will receive after
the particular judgment are ...., ...,
or .... (161)

4. In purgatory our soul is .... before we
are able .... (162)

5. When Jesus returns with power as Judge he will .... to the Father. (163)

6. On the day of the last judgment all of us will ...., so that each one may receive ...., according to what .... good or evil. (164)

7. Those who have done evil and turned from God will .... and will .... and will be .... forever. (165)

8. Those who have done good will .... and will receive the reward of .... (166)

9. During our life on earth we should .... and............. God faithfully so that we may .... and ...... in eternal life in heaven. (167)

CAN YOU ANSWER THESE?

1. When shall we be reunited with God? (159)

2. What is the particular judgment? (160)

3. What will happen after the particular judgment? (161)

4. Why do some souls go to purgatory? (162)

5. What will Jesus do at the last judgment? (163)

6. What will happen after the last judgment? (164)

7. How will evil people be punished? (165)

8. What will be the reward of those who have done right in life? (166)

9. How can we get ready for our death? (167)

THE LAST JUDGMENT

SHORTLY before he ate the last Passover meal with his disciples Jesus said, "When the Son of Man comes as King and all the angels with him, he will sit on his royal throne, and the people of all the nations will be gathered before him. Then he will divide them into two groups, just as a shepherd separates the sheep from the goats. He will put the good people at his right and the others at his left.

Jesus will return in power as Judge

"Then the King will say to the people on his right, 'Come, you that are blessed by my Father! Come and possess the kingdom which has been prepared for you ever since the creation of the world. I was hungry and you fed me, thirsty and you gave me a drink; I was a stranger and you received me in your homes, naked and you clothed me; I was sick and you took care of me, in prison and you visited me.'

"The good people will then answer him, 'When, Lord, did we ever see you hungry and feed you, or thirsty and give you a drink? When did we ever see you a stranger and welcome you in our homes, nor naked and clothe you? When did we ever see you sick or in prison, and visit you?'

"The King will reply, 'I tell you, whenever you did this for one of the least important of these brothers of mine, you did it for me.'

"The bad people will be sent off to eternal punishment, but the good people will go to eternal life."

Appendices

Author's Note: It is important that parents and teachers be aware of the following directive:

> In every age and culture Christianity has commended certain prayers, formulas, and practices to all members of the faith community, even the youngest. While catechesis cannot be limited to the repetition of formulas and it is essential that formulas and facts pertaining to faith be understood, memorization has nevertheless had a special place in the handing-on of the faith throughout the ages and should continue to have such a place today, especially in catechetical programs for the young. It should be adapted to the level and ability of the child and introduced in a gradual manner, through a process which, begun early, continues gradually, flexibly, and never slavishly. In this way certain elements of Catholic faith, tradition, and practice are learned for a lifetime and can contribute to the individual's continued growth in understanding and living the faith.
>
> Among these are the following:
>
> 1. Prayers such as the Sign of the Cross, Lord's Prayer, Hail Mary, Apostles' Creed, Acts of Faith, Hope and Charity, Act of Contrition.
>
> 2. Factual information contributing to an appreciation of the place of the word of God in the Church and the life of the Christian through an awareness and understanding of: the key themes of the history of salvation; the major personalities of the Old and New Testaments; and certain biblical texts expressive of God's love and care.
>
> 3. Formulas providing factual information regarding worship, the Church Year, and major feasts of our Lord and our Lady, the various eucharistic devotions, the mysteries of the rosary of the Blessed Virgin Mary, and the Stations of the Cross.
>
> 4. Formulas and practices dealing with the moral life of Christians including the commandments, the beatitudes, the gifts of the Holy Spirit, the theological and moral virtues, the precepts of the Church, and the examination of conscience.   (*National Catechetical Directory,*176e)

APPENDIX 1
ESSENTIAL PRAYERS

Sign of the Cross

IN the name of the Father, and the Son, and of the Holy Spirit. Amen.

The Lord's Prayer

OUR Father, who art in heaven, hallowed be thy name; thy kingdom come; thy will be done on earth as it is in heaven. Give us this day our daily bread; and forgive us our trespasses as we forgive those who trespass against us; and lead us not into temptation, but deliver us from evil. Amen.

Hail Mary

HAIL Mary, full of grace! The Lord is with you; blessed are you among women, and blessed is the fruit of your womb, Jesus. Holy Mary, Mother of God, pray for us sinners, now and at the hour of our death. Amen.

Doxology

GLORY be to the Father, and to the Son and to the Holy Spirit. As it was in the beginning, is now, and ever shall be, world without end. Amen.

The Apostles' Creed

I BELIEVE in God the Father Almighty, Creator of heaven and earth; And in Jesus Christ, his only Son, our Lord; who was conceived by the Holy Spirit, born of the Virgin Mary; suffered under Pontius Pilate, was crucified, died, and was buried; he descended into hell; the third day he rose again from the dead; he ascended into heaven, and sits at the right hand of God the Father Almighty; from thence he shall come to judge the living and the dead. I believe in the Holy Spirit; the Holy Catholic Church; the Communion of Saints; the forgiveness of sins; the resurrection of the body; and life everlasting. Amen.

Act of Faith

O MY God, I firmly believe all the truths that the holy Catholic Church believes and teaches; I believe these truths, O Lord, because you, the infallible Truth, have revealed them to her; in this faith I am resolved to live and die. Amen.

Act of Hope

O MY God, trusting in your promises, and because you are faithful, powerful and merciful, I hope, through the merits of Christ, for the pardon of my sins, final perseverance, and the blessed glory of heaven. Amen.

Act of Charity

O MY God, because you are infinite Goodness and worthy of infinite love, I love you with my whole heart above all things, and for love of you, I love my fellowmen as myself. Amen.

Act of Contrition

O MY God, I am heartily sorry for having offended you, and I detest all my sins, because of your just punishments, but most of all because they offend you, my God, who are all good and deserving of all my love. I firmly resolve, with the help of your grace, to sin no more and to avoid the near occasions of sin.

Hail, Holy Queen

HAIL, holy Queen, Mother of mercy; hail our life, our sweetness, and our hope. To you do we cry, poor banished children of Eve. To you do we send up our sighs, mourning and weeping in this valley of tears. Turn then, most gracious Advocate, your eyes of mercy toward us. And after this our exile show unto us the blessed fruit of your womb, Jesus. O clement, O loving, O sweet Virgin Mary.

The Angelus

THE Angel of the Lord declared to Mary
And she conceived by the Holy Spirit. Hail Mary . . .
Behold the handmaid of the Lord.
Be it done to me according to your word. Hail Mary . . .
And the Word was made flesh.
And dwelt among us. Hail Mary . . .
Pray for us, O holy Mother of God.
That we may be made worthy of the promises of Christ.

Let us pray

POUR forth, we beseech you, O Lord, your grace into our hearts; that as we have known the incarnation of Christ, your Son, by the message of the angel, so by his Passion and Cross, we may be brought to the glory of his resurrection. Through the same Christ our Lord. Amen.

Grace before Meals

BLESS us, O Lord, and these your gifts which we are about to receive from your bounty. Through Christ our Lord. Amen.

Grace after Meals

WE give you thanks, Almighty God, for all your benefits, who live and reign world without end. Amen.

APPENDIX 2
THE HOLY BIBLE

"THE BIBLE IS THE WORD OF GOD ... IN THE LANGUAGE OF MAN"

- *What is the Bible?*

The Bible is a collection of sacred books, which were composed under the positive influence of the Holy Spirit by men chosen by God, and which have been accepted by the Church as inspired.

- *Who is the principal author of the Bible?*

God is the principal author of the Bible.

- *When and where was the Bible written?*

The Bible was written at various times and at various places by men chosen for this purpose by God.

- *How many books are in the Bible?*

In the Bible, as we know it, there are seventy-three books; forty-six books are in the Old Testament and twenty-seven in the New Testament.

- *If the Bible is written by men, why do we say that it is the Word of God?*

We say that the Bible is the Word of God because God inspired the men who wrote it.

- *Why is the Bible more excellent than any other book?*

The Bible is more excellent than any other book because God is its author and it centers around the mystery of the redemption of man.

- *How is the Old Testament related to the mystery of the redemption?*

The Old Testament describes the remote preparation for the coming of the Messiah.

- *Who are some of the outstanding people in the Old Testament?*

Abraham, our father in the faith; Moses, leader of God's people; David, King and Psalmist; and Isaiah, the Prophet of the Messiah.

● *How is the New Testament related to the mystery of the redemption?*

The New Testament describes the nature of the Messiah and tells the story of His redemptive mission.

● *Who are some of the outstanding people of the New Testament?*

Jesus Christ, the Son of God; Mary, his Virgin Mother; Peter, the Head of Christ's Church; and Paul, the Apostle who brought the Church to all people.

● *Can we really know and love Christ unless we study the Bible?*

No, we cannot know and love Christ unless we study the Bible because as Saint Augustine has said: "The New Testament is hidden in the Old Testament, and the Old Testament throws light on the New." Saint Jerome said: "Not to know the Bible is not to know Christ."

APPENDIX 3

THE LITURGY

The Church Year

EACH year through the Liturgy (especially the Mass), the Church makes present for us the Life, Death, and Resurrection of Jesus. In this way, we can encounter our Lord in his Mysteries, give glory to God, and obtain graces for ourselves and the whole world.

Outline of the Church Year

Advent — *Jesus is near.*
Christmas — *Jesus is with us.*
Epiphany — *Jesus shows his glory.*
Ordinary Time — *Jesus gives lessons for his Church.*
Lent — *Jesus suffers and dies for us.*
Easter — *Jesus triumphs over sin and death.*
Easter Time — *Jesus instructs his apostles.*
Ascension — *Jesus ascends to his heavenly Father.*
Pentecost — *Jesus sends the Holy Spirit.*
Ordinary Time — *The Spirit carries on the work of Jesus through his Church.*

Holy Mass

ON the Cross Jesus offered his body and blood to God the Father for us. In the Mass this great act is renewed for our benefit. We offer Jesus to God the Father in adoration, thanksgiving, reparation, and petition. We receive Jesus back from the Father as our Bread for eternal life. We sing hymns to praise God and to show our joy at Mass.

Major Parts of Holy Mass

Introductory Rites — *We speak to God in acts of contrition, praise, and petition.*

Liturgy of the Word — *We listen to what God says to us in the Readings, the Gospel, and the Homily.*

Liturgy of the Eucharist —

    Preparation of the Gifts — *With the priest we present the gifts of bread and wine.*

    Eucharistic Prayer — *At the consecration this bread and wine are changed into the Body and Blood of Jesus.*

    Communion Rite — *We receive Jesus who has given himself in love.*

Concluding Rite — *We receive God's blessing and go forth to bring Jesus to others.*

The Seven Sacraments

Baptism	Anointing of the Sick
Confirmation	Holy Orders
Holy Eucharist	Matrimony
Penance	

Holy Days of Obligation in the United States

All Sundays of the year
January 1—Solemnity of Mary, Mother of God
Ascension of our Lord (forty days after Easter)
August 15—Assumption of the Blessed Virgin Mary
November 1—All Saints' Day
December 8—The Immaculate Conception
December 25—Christmas Day.

Major Feasts of Jesus and Mary

The major events of the Redemption are recalled in the feasts of Christ and find echoes in the feasts of Mary.

Jesus	*Mary*
Annunciation (Mar. 25)	— Immaculate Conception (Dec. 8)
Birth (Dec. 25)	— Birth (Sept. 8)
Presentation (Feb. 2)	— Presentation (Nov. 21)
Passion and Death (holy Week)	— Seven Sorrows (Sept. 15)
Resurrection (Easter Sun.)	— Assumption (Aug. 15)
Kingship (Last Sun. of Year)	— Queenship (Aug. 22)
Sacred Heart (Friday after Corpus Christi)	— Immaculate Heart (Saturday after Sacred Heart)
Body of Christ (Corpus Christi) (Sunday after Pentecost)	— Motherhood of Mary (Jan. 1)

Devotions to the Blessed Sacrament

AFTER Mass, Jesus remains in the tabernacles of our churches so that the sick who could not be present at Mass may also receive him. He also is there to receive our adoration in the rite of Benediction of the Blessed Sacrament. Finally, he is there so that we can visit him and draw strength and consolation from his presence.

The Mysteries of the Rosary

The Joyful Mysteries
1. The Annunciation of the Archangel Gabriel to Mary.
2. The Visitation of the Virgin Mary.
3. The Birth of Our Lord at Bethlehem.
4. The Presentation of Our Lord in the Temple.
5. The Finding of Our Lord in the Temple.

The Sorrowful Mysteries
1. The Agony of Our Lord in Garden of Gethsemane.
2. The Scourging of Our Lord at the pillar.
3. The crowning of Our Lord with thorns.
4. The carrying of the Cross by Our Lord to Calvary.
5. The Crucifixion and Death of Our Lord.

The Glorious Mysteries
1. The Resurrection of Our Lord from the dead.
2. The Ascension of Our Lord into Heaven.
3. Descent of the Holy Spirit upon the Apostles.
4. The Assumption of Mary into Heaven.
5. Crowning of Mary as Queen of Heaven.

Stations of the Cross

1. Pilate condemns Jesus.
2. Jesus takes his cross.
3. Jesus falls to the ground for the first time.
4. Jesus meets his Mother.
5. Simon helps Jesus carry his cross.
6. Veronica wipes the face of Jesus.
7. Jesus falls for the second time.
8. Jesus meets the women of Jerusalem.
9. Jesus falls for the third time.
10. The soldiers tear off Jesus' clothes.
11. Jesus is nailed to the cross.
12. Jesus dies on the cross.
13. Jesus is taken from the cross.
14. Jesus is laid in the tomb.

APPENDIX 4

CHRISTIAN LIVING

The Ten Commandments of God

1. I, the Lord, am your God. You shall not have other gods besides me.
2. You shall not take the name of the Lord, your God in vain.
3. Remember to keep holy the sabbath day.
4. Honor your father and mother.
5. You shall not kill.
6. You shall not commit adultery.
7. You shall not steal.
8. You shall not bear false witness against your neighbor.
9. You shall not covet your neighbor's wife.
10. You shall not covet anything that belongs to your neighbor.

Duties of Catholics

Chief Precepts of the Church

1. To keep holy the day of the Lord's Resurrection: to worship God by participating in Mass every Sunday and holyday of obligation: to avoid those activities that would hinder renewal of soul and body, e.g., needless work and business activities, unnecessary shopping and so on.
2. To lead a sacramental life: to receive Holy Communion frequently and the Sacrament of Penance—minimally, to receive

the Sacrament fo Penance at least once a year (annual confession is obligatory).

—minimally also, to receive Holy Communion at least once a year, between the First Sunday of Lent and Trinity Sunday.

3. To study Catholic teaching in preparation for the Sacrament of Confirmation, to be confirmed, and then to continue to study and advance the cause of Christ.

4. To observe the marriage laws of the Church: to give religious training, by example and word, to one's children; to use parish schools and catechical programs.

5. To strengthen and support the Church: one's own parish community and parish priests, the worldwide Church and the Pope.

6. To do penance, including abstaining from meat and fasting from food on the appointed days.

7. To join in the missionary spirit and apostolate of the Church.

The Beatitudes

1. Blest are the poor in spirit: the reign of God is theirs.
2. Blest are the sorrowing: they shall be consoled.
3. Blest are the lowly: they shall inherit the land.
4. Blest are they who hunger and thirst for holiness: they shall have their fill.
5. Blest are they who show mercy: mercy shall be theirs.
6. Blest are the single-hearted: for they shall see God.
7. Blest are the peacemakers: they shall be called sons of God.
8. Blest are those persecuted for holiness' sake: the reign of God is theirs. (Mt 5:3-10)

The Seven Gifts of the Holy Spirit

Wisdom, Understanding, Counsel, Fortitude, Knowledge, Piety, Fear of the Lord.

The Theological Virtues

FAITH is a gift by which the Holy Spirit helps us to accept God's word and to give ourselves to the Father.

HOPE is a gift which helps us to know God that loves us and cares for us and that we can trust in him.

LOVE is a gift which helps us to love God and to love all people for the love of God because they too belong to him.

The Moral Virtues

PRUDENCE disposes us to form right judgments about what we must do or not do.

JUSTICE disposes us to give everyone what belongs to him.

FORTITUDE disposes us to do what is good in spite of any difficulty.

TEMPERANCE disposes us to control our desires and to use rightly the things which please our senses.

Examination of Conscience

First Commandment:
> Have I neglected my morning or night prayers?
> Have I misbehaved at Mass?

Second Commandment
> Have I used God's name irreverently?

Third Commandment:
> Have I missed Mass through my own fault on Sundays or holydays?

Fourth Commandment:
> Have I disobeyed, angered, or been disrespectful toward my parents or teachers?

Fifth Commandment:
> Have I quarreled with or willfully hurt anyone?
> Have I refused to forgive?
> Have I caused another to commit sin?

Sixth and Ninth Commandments:
> Have I offended in any way by thought, word, or deed against the virtue of purity?

Seventh and Tenth Commandments:
> Have I stolen or destroyed property belonging to any other person?
> Have I knowingly accepted stolen goods?

Eighth Commandment:
> Have I told lies or injured another person's character?

Capital Sins:
> Have I been angry, greedy, proud, envious, jealous, lazy. immodest, intemperate in eating or drinking?